The Dog in the Fog

By Cameron Macintosh

Pen and Jet go for a jog.

Jet runs to a pit!

He has fun in the mud.

Dig, dig, dig!

Jet sits up.

He sees a rat!

Jet runs off to get the rat.

The rat runs in to the fog.

Pen can not see Jet.

Pen runs in to the fog.

Pen runs to get a pot.

Pen hits the pot.

Jet runs to Pen!

CHECKING FOR MEANING

1. What did Jet do at the pit? *(Literal)*

2. Why did Jet run into the fog? *(Literal)*

3. How did Jet know where to find Pen? *(Inferential)*

EXTENDING VOCABULARY

get	Look at the word *get*. What other words can you make by changing the first letter of this word? E.g. let, met, net, pet, set, wet.
not	Explain that the word *not* can help to make opposites in the story, e.g. *not* see. Think of other words that can be used with *not* to make opposites, e.g. *not* run, *not* go, *not* dig.
pot	What is a *pot*? What is a pot used for? What are the three sounds in this word?

MOVING BEYOND THE TEXT

1. How does it feel to be in fog? Is it hot or cold, wet or dry, fun or scary?

2. How would Jet have felt when he couldn't find Pen?

3. If Pen and Jet go jogging again, what could Pen do to keep Jet safe?

4. What other types of weather can you describe?

SPEED SOUNDS

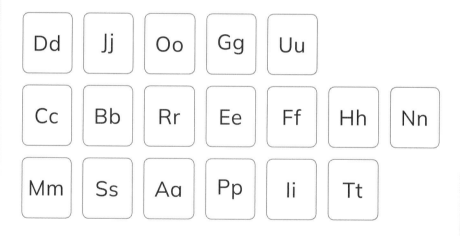

Dd	Jj	Oo	Gg	Uu

Cc	Bb	Rr	Ee	Ff	Hh	Nn

Mm	Ss	Aa	Pp	Ii	Tt

PRACTICE WORDS

Jet

jog

runs

dig

fun

fog

not

up

mud

get

pot

and

off

Dig